# PETER

## LEARNING TO
## BE LIKE JESUS

ROBBIE
CASTLEMAN

12 STUDIES
FOR INDIVIDUALS
OR GROUPS

ivp

Life

Builder

Study

INTER-VARSITY PRESS
36 Causton Street, London SW1P 4ST, England
*Email: ivp@ivpbooks.com*
*Website: www.ivpbooks.com*

© Robbie Castleman, 1999
First UK edition © Scripture Union, 1999
This edition © Inter-Varsity Press, 2018

*Originally published in the United States of America in the LifeGuide® Bible Studies series
in 1999 by InterVarsity Press, Downers Grove, Illinois*
*First published in Great Britain by Scripture Union in 1999*
*This edition published in Great Britain by Inter-Varsity Press 2018*

**British Library Cataloguing-in-Publication Data**
A catalogue record for this book is available from the British Library.

ISBN: 978–1–78359–807–6

Printed in Great Britain by Ashford Colour Press Ltd, Gosport, Hampshire

*Inter-Varsity Press publishes Christian books that are true to the Bible and that
communicate the gospel, develop discipleship and strengthen the church for its mission
in the world.*

*IVP originated within the Inter-Varsity Fellowship, now the Universities and Colleges
Christian Fellowship, a student movement connecting Christian Unions in universities
and colleges throughout Great Britain, and a member movement of the International
Fellowship of Evangelical Students. Website: www.uccf.org.uk. That historic association
is maintained, and all senior IVP staff and committee members subscribe to the UCCF
Basis of Faith.*

# Contents

# Getting the Most Out of *Peter*

Simon Peter is a contradiction in terms—like loud silence or dark light. This impetuous fisherman is a contradiction who illustrates what happens when God touches someone and he or she is forever changed.

Simon Peter walked on the water and then sank in it. He was the first to confess that Jesus is the Son of God and five minutes later tried to tell Jesus what to do. He promised to lay down his life for Jesus—and within a day denied three times that he ever knew him! He risked his reputation to share the gospel with Gentiles but later refused to eat with them. He was called to be a fisher of human beings, but he was more comfortable fishing for fish. His last catch of fish numbered 153. His first sermon harvested 3,000 souls.

Jesus changed Simon Peter's name and his self–image, his profession and his prejudices. Jesus changed his expectations and priorities, his family life and prayer petitions. Jesus changed Peter. Completely.

Simon Peter is an illustration of God's promise in Philippians 1:6: God, "who began a good work in you will carry it on to completion until the day of Christ Jesus." Simon Peter shows us that God's good work is not without pain, risk and hard lessons—nor is it without great joy. I am grateful that Simon Peter lived his life out in the open, "on his sleeve," so that we can learn from him how to be more like Jesus day by day.

When God enters the human person, a radical shift takes place. We are a "new creation" (2 Cor 5:17). Simon Peter shows us how, as people transformed by God in our deepest being, we can grow to be who we really are in Christ Jesus. I pray that these studies will be used by God as a part of his "good work" to change you, to help "bring you to completion" as day by day you grow to be more like Jesus.

## Suggestions for Individual Study

1. As you begin each study, pray that God will speak to you through his Word.

2. Read the introduction to the study and respond to the "personal reflection" question or exercise. This is designed to help you focus on God and on the theme of the study.

3. Each study deals with a particular passage—so that you can delve into the author's meaning in that context. Read and reread the passage to be studied. If you are studying a book, it will be helpful to read through the entire book prior to the first study. The questions are written using the language of the New International Version, so you may wish to use that version of the Bible. The New Revised Standard Version is also recommended.

4. This is an inductive Bible study, designed to help you discover for yourself what Scripture is saying. The study includes three types of questions. *Observation* questions ask about the basic facts: who, what, when, where and how. *Interpretation* questions delve into the meaning of the passage. *Application* questions help you discover the implications of the text for growing in Christ. These three keys unlock the treasures of Scripture.

Write your answers to the questions in the spaces provided or in a personal journal. Writing can bring clarity and deeper understanding of your self and of God's Word.

5. It might be good to have a Bible dictionary handy. Use it to look up any unfamiliar words, names or places.

6. Use the prayer suggestion to guide you in thanking God for what you have learned and to pray about the applications that have come to mind.

7. You may want to go on to the suggestion under "Now or Later," or you may want to use that idea for your next study.

## Suggestions for Members of a Group Study

1. Come to the study prepared. Follow the suggestions for individual study mentioned above. You will find that careful preparation will greatly enrich your time spent in group discussion.

2. Be willing to participate in the discussion. The leader of your group will not be lecturing. Instead, he or she will be encouraging the

members of the group to discuss what they have learned. The leader will be asking the questions that are found in this guide.

3. Stick to the topic being discussed. Your answers should be based on the verses which are the focus of the discussion and not on outside authorities such as commentaries or speakers. These studies focus on a particular passage of Scripture. Only rarely should you refer to other portions of the Bible. This allows for everyone to participate in in-depth study on equal ground.

4. Be sensitive to the other members of the group. Listen attentively when they describe what they have learned. You may be surprised by their insights! Each question assumes a variety of answers. Many questions do not have "right" answers, particularly questions that aim at meaning or application. Instead the questions push us to explore the passage more thoroughly.

   When possible, link what you say to the comments of others. Also be affirming whenever you can. This will encourage some of the more hesitant members of the group to participate.

5. Be careful not to dominate the discussion. We are sometimes so eager to express our thoughts that we leave too little opportunity for others to respond. By all means participate! But allow others to also.

6. Expect God to teach you through the passage being discussed and through the other members of the group. Pray that you will have an enjoyable and profitable time together, but also that as a result of the study, you will find ways that you can take action individually and/ or as a group.

7. Remember that anything said in the group is considered confidential and should not be discussed outside the group unless specific permission is given to do so.

8. If you are the group leader, you will find additional suggestions at the back of the guide.

# 1

# Learning to Obey

## Luke 5:1–11

From the toddler who says, "No!" to an athlete refusing a coach's direction, people are prone to disobey authority. Learning to obey God is essential to a Christian's life of faith.

GROUP DISCUSSION. Write on a piece of paper, in one or two sentences, a summary of the most difficult thing God ever asked you to do. Fold the papers and put all of them together for a random drawing. Read each one and try to guess who wrote it. Then talk about what you felt or thought about as you tried to be obedient to God at that time.

PERSONAL REFLECTION. Think about times when obedience to God has been particularly challenging or difficult. What areas of your life or particular situations or people cause the most struggle for you?

Early in Jesus' ministry, most of his followers maintained their jobs, homes and businesses. Eventually Jesus called a few to leave their homes and jobs indefinitely to help him in his ministry. Luke's Gospel tells us how this challenge came to Simon Peter. We will see how Peter struggled to obey the word of the Lord—especially in an area of his life where he was an "expert"! *Read Luke 5:1–11.*

1. Describe the setting, including the crowd, sights, sounds, smells, time of day and what the fishermen were doing.

2. If Jesus' teaching was illustrated by his command to Peter and the miracle that followed, what do you think Jesus was teaching?

3. What objection did Simon include in his response to Jesus' request (vv. 4–5)?

4. If you had been a part of the crowd on this unusual morning, how do you think you might have reacted to the events in verses 5–10?

5. What do you think prompted Simon's confession of sinfulness to Jesus (v. 8)?

6. Notice how Jesus responded to Simon (v. 10). What are other ways Jesus could have responded?

7. When you have felt unworthy or have had reasons for feeling guilty, how have you responded to the grace of God extended to you?

8. How is the call to tell others about Jesus appropriate—both to Simon and to us—when we recognize how sinful we are?

---

9. How do you feel about being called to evangelism?

---

10. Why might this have been a particularly difficult time for these fishermen to leave everything and follow Jesus?

---

11. Simon was an "expert" fisherman; fishing was what he knew and was good at. Why are personal areas of strength and know-how often difficult areas of obedience to the Lord?

---

12. Personal failure in an area of strength (they fished all night and caught nothing, v. 5) often precedes an opportunity to obey the Lord in a new way. How have you experienced this in your life?

*Pray that you will become more obedient to God.*

## Now or Later

Think about a particular area of disobedience to God and his Word (or area where you struggle with being obedient). Confess this to someone you trust to pray for you and help you grow in obedience to the Lord.

# 2

# Learning to Pray

Jesus had to make daily decisions in his public ministry that influenced his work and his followers. The demands of limited time, overwhelming needs and the expectations of others were all realities for Jesus as they are for us.

GROUP DISCUSSION. Briefly summarize a recent major decision you had to make, describing how that decision was reached and what helped in making the choice.

PERSONAL REFLECTION. Think about several major decisions you have made over the last several years. What did you find helpful in making these decisions? What hindrances were encountered in the same process?

Prayer is an essential part of learning to be like Jesus. In this study we see Jesus in action—healing and teaching. And these events are bracketed by prayer. *Read Mark 1:29–39.*

1. Describe the events in these verses from Simon Peter's perspective.

2. How would you respond if "the whole town" of sick and distressed people gathered at your door (v. 33)?

_____

3. How would Jesus' practice of going to pray alone (v. 35) affect the way he made decisions?

_____

4. Describe Jesus' response to Simon Peter's request (vv. 36–38).

_____

5. Considering what happened just before and right after Jesus' time of prayer, what do you think he prayed about?

_____

6. Summarize your personal habits of prayer (time, place, routine).

How has prayer made a difference to you during stressful times in your life?

_____

7. *Read Luke 6:12–23.* Compare the circumstances of this prayer to the one just studied in Mark. What do you think was Jesus' concern for this particular prayer time?

8. If you were directing a movie, how would you stage the scene beginning in verse 17?

9. Notice in verse 20 that Jesus is addressing the disciples while speaking to this large crowd. What do you think Jesus communicated to the disciples in his sermon in contrast to this situation?

10. How might Jesus' sermon encourage or discourage Simon Peter and the other disciples?

11. Consider your own habits of prayer in light of Jesus' patterns of prayer. How do your habits help or hinder your ability to make wise choices as you serve God?

*Pray about current and specific situations, decisions and concerns in your life.*

### Now or Later

Make specific plans to improve the habits of your prayer life. If needed, think about how to set aside a specific time and place for prayer. Reading a book about prayer or a book of prayers can also be helpful.

# 3

# Learning to Trust

## Matthew 14:22–34

Learning to "walk by faith and not by sight" is a challenge to trust the Lord more than we trust ourselves.

GROUP DISCUSSION. When have difficult circumstances discouraged your ability to trust God?

Begin the study with a time of prayer that God's Word will deepen and mature each person's trust in the Lord.

PERSONAL REFLECTION. Write a letter to the Lord about a situation when you began well in placing your trust in him, but as circumstances became more difficult, your ability to trust God failed or wavered. Pray that the Lord will use this study to make your faith in him stronger.

Peter's "shaping" continues as he and the other disciples encounter a severe storm on the sea at a time when Jesus was not with them. However, the Lord does not leave them alone in their trouble and uses this experience as a "teachable moment" in Peter's life. *Read Matthew 14:22–34.*

1. Jesus had just fed five-thousand-plus people with five loaves of bread and two fish (vv. 15–21). How did Jesus' actions in verses 22–23 reflect what he was thinking and feeling at this time?

2. How do you think the disciples were feeling in verses 22–24?

_____

3. How did the disciples react when Jesus walked on the water (vv. 25-26)? Why?

_____

4. What important information do you find in Jesus' response to them?

_____

5. What are some possible reasons for Peter's request in verse 28?

Why do you think Jesus responded to Peter the way he did (v. 29)?

_____

6. Do you think Peter was surprised at the Lord's positive response to his request? Why or why not?

_____

7. What emotions would Peter have experienced while walking, sinking and being rescued (vv. 29–31)?

8. In what ways do we walk by sight and not by faith like Peter did here?

9. When Jesus asked, "Why did you doubt?" (v. 31), what reasons might Peter have given Jesus to account for his lack of faith?

10. Look at verses 32–33. What did Peter and the other disciples learn about Jesus from this experience?

11. List some things that tend to overwhelm your ability to trust the Lord.

12. How can Scripture, Jesus' voice today, help you trust God in turbulent or threatening times?

*Take time at the close of this study to worship the Lord in prayer, giving to him the past or present situations that came to mind at the beginning.*

### Now or Later

Make a list of important points to consider in preparing for trusting God for the future, identifying what makes you more prone to doubt as well as what helps you trust the Lord.

# 4

# Learning to Believe

## Matthew 16:13–25

Who was this incredible person Peter had chosen to follow? Understanding who Jesus is is essential to knowing what Jesus would do. Learning to be like Jesus has everything to do with who we believe Jesus to be.

GROUP DISCUSSION. If a TV reporter asked you, "Who do you think Jesus is?" what would you say? Take several minutes and write down on a piece of paper your one-minute response to this question. Then have each person read what they have written.

PERSONAL REFLECTION. Think of a friend, family member or child who does not yet know the Lord in a personal way. If they were to ask you, "So, who is Jesus?" what would you say? Write a paragraph stating your reply. Then take time to pray for the person you had in mind as you wrote. Ask the Lord to prepare their hearts to know who Jesus is and for an opportunity to help them understand how Scripture defines who Jesus is.

The Scriptures that lead up to today's passage record several encounters between Jesus and people who had very different ideas about who he was. In this study, Jesus takes advantage of all the rumors about him to talk to his followers about who he is. *Read Matthew 16:13–25.*

1. In response to Jesus' question in verse 13, how do the disciples summarize the popular opinions about who Jesus is (v. 14)?

2. C.S. Lewis summarized the possible identity of Jesus by saying he was either "a liar, a lunatic or the Lord." How does believing Jesus to be the Lord make a difference in your life?

3. What were the two ideas about Jesus that Peter offered and how are they distinct from what had been said before (v. 16)?

4. List the various things Jesus included in his response to Simon Peter's statement (vv. 17–20).

5. Jesus addressed Peter directly as "Simon son of Jonah." In light of Jesus' comments about the establishment of the church (v. 18), how might this connect with the story of Jonah in the Old Testament?

6. Notice Jesus' warning in verse 26. From the context of the passage and other opinions in verse 14, why do you think Jesus gives such a warning?

7. How does your knowledge of who Jesus really is affect your work and your witness?

8. Note how Jesus begins at this point in his ministry to define his ministry in different terms (v 21). Why would this come after Peter's identification of Jesus?

9. How does Peter's response to Jesus' new teaching probably reflect the disciples' feelings as a whole (v. 23)? (Think about how you would have felt if you had been a disciple traveling with Jesus at the time.)

10. Contrast Peter's declarations in verses 16 and then 22. What does the difference in tone indicate about how Peter's opinion of himself might have changed?

11. Describe the challenge Jesus presents to Peter and the other disciples (vv. 23–25).

12. In your own experience, how do knowing who Jesus is and trusting Jesus become disconnected?

What would change in your life if this were a more constant and conscious consideration?

*Ask God to narrow the gap between what you know about Jesus and what you truly believe about him.*

## Now or Later

Identify several situations—practical, ethical, political, personal—where you ask yourself, "What would Jesus do?" Answer each question by thinking about who Jesus *is* in each situation.

# 5

# Learning to Follow

Peter emerged as the spokesman for the disciples. He was often the one who asked Jesus questions and worked to understand him and his purposes. Understanding sometimes meant seeing Jesus in a whole new light.

GROUP DISCUSSION. What are some of the costs of following Christ that we face today (consider your own cultural context and other cultures as well)?

PERSONAL REFLECTION. What has being a Christian cost you? Take several minutes to think, pray or write about your thoughts and feelings concerning the sacrifices you have made in living the life of a Christian.

In this study, we will look at two passages where Simon Peter is confronted by who Jesus is and then challenged by what Jesus demands. *Read Matthew 17:1–8.*

1. If you had been on the mountain with Jesus, what would you have seen and heard?

2. Why do you think Jesus took only the disciples noted in verse 1 up the mountain?

3. Keeping in mind that Jesus had just revealed his plan to suffer and die (16:21–28), what do you imagine Jesus' conversation with Moses and Elijah would have included?

4. How did Peter respond to this experience in verse 4 and why?

5. What is God communicating to the disciples (v. 5)?

6. How did the three disciples respond to God's message?

7. At what times of your life have you responded to Jesus as Peter did?

8. Shortly after the transfiguration Jesus began to teach about the character of his kingdom. *Read Matthew 19:23–30*. The Jews considered material prosperity to be an indication of God's blessing. How did Jesus turn this teaching upside down (v. 29)?

9. Describe the disciples' response to Jesus' teaching.



10. What concern is evident in Peter's response in verse 27?



11. What effect would Jesus' reply (vv. 28–30) have on Peter and the other disciples?



12. Imagine Jesus speaking the words of verses 28–30 to you. How would you feel?



13. How have you received back "many times" what you have lost in your life as a result of following Jesus?



*These passages offer hope and promise as well as demand and sacrifice. Close the study with a time of prayer and praise in response to Jesus.*

**Now or Later**

Read Matthew 18:21–22, another time when Peter asked Jesus a question in his desire to learn to be a disciple. Consider how forgiveness is a mark of God's kingdom and a cost-with-a-promise to kingdom citizens.

# 6

# Learning to Serve

## John 13:1–17

Serving others sacrificially is often the best way to love God—and the hardest part of being a Christian.

GROUP DISCUSSION. Are you more comfortable serving or being served? Why?

PERSONAL REFLECTION. When have you resisted someone's desire to serve you? Think about the circumstances and consider why it was so hard to be served.

Jesus taught his disciples crucial things in his final days. Peter and his fellow-disciples had much to learn about what it means to belong to each other as well as to God. *Read John 13:1–17.*

1. What important facts do you discover about the context, mood and setting of this event?

2. Why did Jesus wash the disciples' feet?

_____

3. How did Simon Peter react to Jesus' attempt to wash his feet and why?

_____

4. What are some reasons some people resist the ministry of Jesus today?

_____

5. Summarize Jesus' response to Peter's protest.

_____

6. Why would it be important for Peter to understand what Jesus was trying to teach and model?

_____

7. Knowing Peter would deny him later, how must Jesus have felt as he washed Peter's feet?

_____

8. What are some of the obstacles and discouragements that we face as individuals and as church members in following Jesus' example today?

9. How does the example of Jesus help in overcoming barriers to service?

_____

10. Jesus washed the feet of all the disciples, including Judas Iscariot. How does this example affect your attitude about serving those who have hurt you?

*In the light of our own sinfulness, the ministry of Jesus is humbling and convicting. Pray about how best to serve those who seem to most need "cleansing."*

## Now or Later

Make a list of possible ministry activities that your group or you and a friend might offer to your church or community. Make plans to follow through on one of these ideas before you finish this study guide.

# 7

# Learning to Love

Promising what we hope for and not what reflects reality can get us into trouble! But these promises often indicate we're at least headed in the right direction. Learning to be like Jesus takes time.

GROUP DISCUSSION. Have each person write on a piece of paper a "tombstone epitaph," a one-line description of their life's notable qualities, without identifying themselves by name. Examples: "Honest business man who loved his wife and kids" or "Faithful friend and pretty good student—she kept her scholarship!" Make this a fun exercise by tossing them into a common basket, having a drawing and trying to guess whose epitaph belongs to whom.

PERSONAL REFLECTION. If you had one week to live, what would you want to do for and say to others?

After eating a last meal with his disciples, Jesus continued to teach his followers—even as he anticipated his impending arrest, trial and death. As Jesus taught his final lessons to the disciples, it was Peter who asked the questions that reflected how the disciples were trying to learn to be like Jesus—with mixed results. *Read John 13:31–14:4.*

1. Knowing that Jesus sensed his time to die was drawing near, what would you have felt during this time if you had been with the twelve?

---

2. How can the focus of Jesus in verses 31 and 32 influence your attitude in loving and serving others?

---

3. What important "last words" and command is Jesus giving to his followers in this passage?

---

4. What particular statement prompted Simon Peter's questions, and why do you think he asked these particular questions?

---

5. Peter makes a promise to Jesus in verse 37. How could Peter's attitude at the time lead to both his making and breaking of the promise?

---

6. Describe Jesus' response (13:38–14:4) and his attitude toward Peter.

---

7. How do you think Peter felt as he listened to Jesus?

8. Contrast Jesus' comments in 13:38 and 14:1–4.

9. How might Jesus' words to Peter and the disciples help you during times of faithfulness or failure?

10. How does Jesus' example affect your understanding of the kind of love commanded of his followers in this passage?

11. How can this exchange between Jesus and Peter help you respond to people who disappoint you with broken promises or weak commitments?

*Part of learning to love, to be like Jesus, is learning to keep good promises. Ask God to help you keep your promises.*

### Now or Later

Reflect back on the footwashing in Study 6. How would Jesus' service of footwashing have affected his teaching in this passage?

# 8

# Learning to Persevere

Learning to be like Jesus is not easy, but it's worth it. Persevering through personal failure, a fallen world, unfaithful friends and uncertain times is essential for our witness as people and communities of faith.

GROUP DISCUSSION. What circumstances make it most difficult for you to be forthright about being a Christian?

PERSONAL REFLECTION. Think about the people you are around who make you uncomfortable as a Christian. What is it about them or your relationship with them that makes witnessing to them difficult?

The hours of Jesus' life continue to move swiftly toward the climax of his ministry While Jesus agonizes and prays in the Garden of Gethsemane, his friends fall asleep. Three times Jesus has to arouse the sleepy disciples to pray with and for him. Finally, Jesus is arrested and taken to the high priest and the Sanhedrin (religious court). Peter follows—keeping his distance. *Read Luke 22:54–62.*

1. Looking throughout the passage, what clues do you have as to how long Peter was in the courtyard?

2. What would have motivated Peter to follow Jesus at all?

Why did he follow "at a distance" (v. 54)?

3. Look at each person who asked Peter about his relationship to Jesus. What do you think prompted their questions?

4. How did Peter's responses reflect changes in his mood and thought as the night progressed?

5. As the cock crowed near dawn, Jesus and Peter looked at each other. Jesus' prophecy in John 13:38 was fulfilled. How do you think Jesus and Peter felt at this moment?

6. Peter had promised to die for Jesus, but found persevering in prayer in the garden and identifying with Jesus in the courtyard difficult. In what ways are you like Peter in your struggle for consistent discipleship?

7. Joseph of Arimathea took Jesus' body from the cross before the Sabbath began and laid it in a tomb. Near dawn the following Sunday, the women followers hurried to prepare Jesus' body for final burial. *Read Luke 24:1–12.*

If you had been a disciple on the way to Jesus' tomb on that morning, what you would have felt (a) on the way to the tomb, (b) after discovering the tomb was empty, (c) as the messengers revealed what had happened, (d) returning from the tomb to tell the twelve disciples and (e) when the disciples refused to believe your account?

8. How was Peter's response to the women's report different from that of the other disciples (v. 12)?

What might this indicate about Peter's attitude toward Jesus—and about himself—since his denial?

9. How does this account of Peter's experiences influence your attitude about important relationships?

about perseverance in prayer?

about personal integrity?

**Now or Later**

Look back at the personal reflection for this study What would it take for you to persevere in your witness to the people who came to mind? (For example, consider praying for them or developing a common interest.) Write down two things you can do and begin to pray about them.

# 9

# Learning to Start Again

## John 21:1–19

Staying busy with familiar tasks is one way people avoid dealing with uncomfortable realities of life. Sticking with the familiar allows us to avoid taking chances and risking failure.

GROUP DISCUSSION. How has dealing with an uncertain situation led to feelings of insecurity for you?

PERSONAL REFLECTION. Think about a particular time when you had to deal with a failed situation or relationship. How did you initially react and how was the situation eventually addressed?

After the resurrection Jesus appeared to his disciples and said, "Peace be with you!" But Thomas struggled with his doubts and Peter was unusually quiet as he remembered his night of denial. Jesus wanted to prepare the disciples well for the time when he would return to his Father. But Peter continued to grieve over his denial of Jesus, and he was unsure of his future as a follower of the Lord. *Read John 21:1–19*.

---

1. After returning home to Galilee, what did Peter decide to do?

Suggest reasons for Peter's decision.

2. Note the similarities to when Peter was first called to be a disciple (Luke 5: 1–11; study one). How is Peter's reaction to the large catch (v. 7) different from the time he fished all night and caught nothing?

3. Note Peter's activity (v. 11). How can "fish-counting" or "keeping busy" be an easy substitute for dealing directly with the Lord?

4. How does Jesus take initiative with Peter in verses 15–20?

5. What do you think "more than these" refers to in Jesus' first question?

6. The first two times Jesus asks Peter about his love, the text uses the Greek word *agape*, a word for unconditional, God-given love. Peter's response to Jesus is recorded using *phileo*, a love of ardent friendship. When Jesus asks Peter the third time, he uses Peter's word, *phileo*, not *agape*. Peter replies using *phileo*, as before. What does the use of different words for love indicate about the relationship between Jesus and Peter?

7. From how Peter responds verbally and emotionally, what would you say Peter has learned about himself?

8. In calling Peter again into his service, Jesus accepted him for who he was and for what he could offer at the time. What significance can this have for your willingness to follow Jesus and serve as a disciple?

_____

9. What did Jesus indicate about the outcome of Peter's willingness to love and follow him (vv. 18–19)? Contrast this situation with the occasion of Peter's promise at the end of John 13 just before his denial.

_____

10. Note how Jesus changes the word for "love" in his third question to match Peter's. How does meeting people where they are help you to be a better friend?

_____

11. What is one "busy" thing you can stop doing to make more time for "being still" and getting to know the Lord better?

*Being honest with God and with ourselves about everything can help keep us from dishonest habits that affect our lives, like busyness or avoidance. Take time to pray about "fish-counting" habits that get in the way of your relationship with the Lord.*

**Now or Later**
Think about how the cost of discipleship affects your response to God's call in your life. How can honesty with God influence your relationship with him?

# 10

# Learning to Witness

## Acts 3:1–20

Learning to be like Jesus is a growing process that can radically change our expectations, comfort zones and life goals.

GROUP DISCUSSION. Talk about a time in your life when God did something for you that you just couldn't keep quiet about.

PERSONAL REFLECTION. Write a "psalm" of thanksgiving to God for a life-changing event in your life.

After commanding the disciples to remain in Jerusalem, Jesus was "taken up" before their eyes (Acts 1). At Pentecost, fifty days after the Sabbath of Passover week when Jesus died, the Holy Spirit came upon the waiting disciples, giving them power to witness to the truth about Jesus. Peter preached to a great crowd on that day and "about three thousand" more people became followers of the risen Lord (Acts 2). Peter had grown profoundly during his three years with Jesus, and now he emerges as the first leader of the new church. *Read Acts 3:1–20.*

---

1. Describe the setting at the temple that afternoon. (Who was present? What were they doing?)

2. What would you have seen happening between Peter, John and the beggar if you were part of the crowd of onlookers?

3. People were accustomed to seeing this beggar at the gate. What similar people and situations do you have in your community?

4. How does Peter describe God in verses 12–14?

Why would this be appropriate for his listeners?

5. What is the central focus of Peter's eyewitness account?

6. How can you prepare to answer people who doubt the resurrection of Jesus is true or historical?

7. Contrast Peter's understanding (v. 18) of Jesus now compared to his rebuke of Jesus in Matthew 16:22 (Study 4).

8. How has your understanding of who Jesus is matured?

9. How can a witnessing community help you be prepared to be a witness to the gospel?

10. The three central ingredients to an eyewitness account of the work of Christ (a testimony) are (1) a reflection on your life before you surrendered to the lordship of Christ, (2) the content of the gospel and how it became clear to you, and (3) how your life has changed and is changing since you have been a follower of the Lord. Write out a brief summary of these things as they relate to your own experience so that you will be prepared to be a witness.

*Take time to pray about areas in your life where you need to be a faithful witness for Christ.*

**Now or Later**

11. Read Acts 4:1–20. Who was most disturbed by Peter's message, and what was the focus of their concern?

12. How would the outcome of Peter's message (v. 4) influence the initial reaction of the Jewish leaders (vv. 13–14)?

13. How did Peter's response to the admonition of the rulers relate to his role as a witness (vv. 19–20)?

# 11

# Learning to Change

Learning to be like Jesus means showing no partiality toward people—no prejudice or racism. These are hard lessons to learn for all of us.

GROUP DISCUSSION. Identify a people-group in your community that is very different from the group gathered for this Bible study. Consider economic, educational, ethnic, cultural and even gender differences.

If God were to ask us to love these folks by sharing the gospel with them and entering into fellowship with them, what might be hard about that? How would we feel about that?

PERSONAL REFLECTION. Identify an area in your life where you struggle with prejudice. What do you think are the roots of this prejudice? What would it take to bring the love of Christ into this relationship? Pray about this and ask the Lord for insight and sensitivity before beginning this study.

The gospel message began to spread in an ever-widening circle as the church scattered from Jerusalem. The church, founded by Jewish believers, began to include faithful Jews beyond Jerusalem and Galilee. All of Palestine was wrestling with the greatness of Jesus. God's people were on the brink of fulfilling their purpose in the world, the promise given to Abraham, that through them the whole world would be blessed.

Peter was a leading ambassador in the missionary adventure of the early church. But he still had some "stretching" to do as he learned to cross cultures for the sake of the gospel. *Read Acts 9:36–10:48.*

1. Peter interacts with a number of different people in 9:36–43. Who were they and what were they like?

2. It was considered "unclean" to touch a dead person if you were a Jewish man, so Peter does not touch Tabitha until she sits up (9:40–41). What does this indicate about Peter's sense of proper religious conduct?

3. Notice that Peter stays at the home of a tanner while residing in Joppa (9:43). A tanner treated the skins of dead animals to make leather goods and was considered unclean in the Jewish community. How do you think you would have felt if you were Peter in this situation?

4. How did staying with Simon the tanner prepare Peter for the events in chapter 10?

5. How is Cornelius described both at the beginning of Acts 10 and by his servants in 10:22?

6. Why do you think Peter had the same vision three times (10:9–16)?

7. Note that Cornelius's servants stopped at the front gate (10:18) and called out for information. Why are these "security guards" (10:7) so cautious?

_____

8. What would make Simon the tanner open his home to these Gentiles and take such a risk in his own community?

_____

9. Describe Peter's journey to Caesarea, his greeting by Cornelius and the scene in his home (10:23–27).

_____

10. What are the major points of Peter's address to Cornelius and his friends?

_____

11. Why would this "second Pentecost" be important for Peter and the Jewish brothers from Joppa to witness?

_____

12. Dealing with racism, prejudice and injustice in the church as well as in the culture is as difficult now as it was in this vivid story of Peter's obedience to crosscultural, religious and racial boundaries. What groups of people would you expect to be unreceptive to the gospel?

13. How have you or a "group" you belong to been excluded by others?

How can that situation help you to be proactive in Jesus' work of reconciliation?

*Pray for a spirit of repentance and a heart and will to be obedient to the Lord's will.*

## Now or Later

It's important to note that Peter crossed the barrier from his side. Read Ephesians 2:11–16. What boundaries can you cross to better understand the "turf" of other people? How might reading novels or other literature help you see the world through the eyes of others very different from you?

# 12

# Learning to Learn

## Acts 15:1–12; Galatians 2:11–16

Some of the best lessons in life are those we have to learn over and over. Some of the hardest lessons are those we thought we had already learned—but then discover we really hadn't. The promise of Scripture is that God "who began a good work in you will bring it to completion in the day of Jesus Christ" (Phil 1:6). And, as with Peter, God will use a lifetime and a community of faithful friends to do just that!

GROUP DISCUSSION. Describe a time when a friend has helped you grow in your Christian life by holding you accountable.

PERSONAL REFLECTION. When have you helped hold someone accountable for something in the Christian life? What was hard about that? What was rewarding? What did you learn in the process?

As more Gentiles came to faith in Jesus, some of the Jewish believers began to impose Jewish traditions and laws on Gentile believers as a prerequisite for salvation. The debate between those who thought this was necessary and those who did not was serious. The church leaders in Jerusalem were asked for a ruling on the matter. Peter was a judge in the center of the controversy. *Read Acts 15:1–12.*

1. Summarize the major parties involved and the issues at stake in the early church as reflected in this passage.


2. When did Peter choose to speak up in the debate? Why?


3. About ten years had passed since Peter's ministry to Cornelius and the Gentiles in Acts 10. How might Peter's "timing" indicate how he had changed from the time he first began to follow Jesus?


4. Summarize Peter's arguments in verses 7–11.


5. What opportunities have you had to address or help settle a dispute concerning biblical truth? What did you do well and what could you have done better in that situation?


6. Peter had made great strides in learning to follow Jesus, but he still had more to learn. In one area where Peter's theology was right but his behavior was wrong, Paul rebuked him. *Read Galatians 2:11–16.* What is Paul's central point concerning Peter's hypocrisy?


7. What fears could Peter have had that led to his compromise?

8. Repentance is often the fruit of a painful rebuke. How does the continuing transformation of Peter affect your attitude toward learning to be like Jesus?

_____

9. In what ways do you struggle with a tendency toward hypocrisy?

Who might help you become more consistent in learning to be like Jesus in this area of your life?

_____

10. Throughout these studies, which characteristic of Peter have you identified with most and why?

_____

11. How has this study of Simon Peter helped you learn to be more like Jesus?

_____

12. What changes would you like to see in your life as you continue learning what it means to be a disciple?

*Pray with thanksgiving for the ways you sense you have grown to be more like Jesus. Pray too for the lessons you will learn on the journey ahead.*

## Now or Later

If you were to write an epitaph for Peter's tomb, what would you write? For example, Here lies Simon Peter, a man who _____.
Write an epitaph for your own life to date. For example, Here is (your name), someone who _____.

# Leader's Notes

*MY GRACE IS SUFFICIENT FOR YOU. (2 COR 12:9)*

Leading a Bible discussion can be an enjoyable and rewarding experience. But it can also be scary—especially if you've never done it before. If this is your feeling, you're in good company. When God asked Moses to lead the Israelites out of Egypt, he replied, "O Lord, please send someone else to do it!" (Ex 4:13). It was the same with Solomon, Jeremiah and Timothy, but God helped these people in spite of their weaknesses, and he will help you as well.

You don't need to be an expert on the Bible or a trained teacher to lead a Bible discussion. The idea behind these inductive studies is that the leader guides group members to discover for themselves what the Bible has to say. This method of learning will allow group members to remember much more of what is said than a lecture would.

These studies are designed to be led easily. As a matter of fact, the flow of questions through the passage from observation to interpretation to application is so natural that you may feel that the studies lead themselves. This study guide is also flexible. You can use it with a variety of groups—student, professional, neighborhood or church groups. Each study takes forty-five to sixty minutes in a group setting.

There are some important facts to know about group dynamics and encouraging discussion. The suggestions listed below should enable you to effectively and enjoyably fulfill your role as leader.

## Preparing for the Study

1. Ask God to help you understand and apply the passage in your own life. Unless this happens, you will not be prepared to lead others. Pray too for the various members of the group. Ask God to open your hearts to the message of his Word and motivate you to action.

2. Read the introduction to the guide to get an overview of the entire book and the issues which will be explored.

3. As you begin each study, read and reread the assigned Bible passage to familiarize yourself with it.

4. This study guide is based on the New International Version of the Bible. It will help you and the group if you use this translation as the basis for your study and discussion.

5. Carefully work through each question in the study. Spend time in meditation and reflection as you consider how to respond.

6. Write your thoughts and responses in the space provided in the study guide. This will help you to express your understanding of the passage clearly.

7. It might help to have a Bible dictionary handy. Use it to look up any unfamiliar words, names or places. (For additional help on how to study a passage, see chapter five of *How to Lead a LifeBuilder Study*, IVP, 2018.)

8. Consider how you can apply the Scripture to your life. Remember that the group will follow your lead in responding to the studies. They will not go any deeper than you do.

9. Once you have finished your own study of the passage, familiarize yourself with the leader's notes for the study you are leading. These are designed to help you in several ways. First, they tell you the purpose the study guide author had in mind when writing the study. Take time to think through how the study questions work together to accomplish that purpose. Second, the notes provide you with additional background information or suggestions on group dynamics for various questions. This information can be useful if people have difficulty understanding or answering a question. Third, the leader's notes can alert you to potential problems you may encounter during the study.

10. If you wish to remind yourself of anything mentioned in the leader's notes, make a note to yourself below that question in the study.

## Leading the Study

1. Begin the study on time. Open with prayer, asking God to help the group to understand and apply the passage.

2. Be sure that everyone in your group has a study guide. Encourage the group to prepare beforehand for each discussion by reading the introduction to the guide and by working through the questions in the study.

3. At the beginning of your first time together, explain that these studies are meant to be discussions, not lectures. Encourage the members of the group to participate. However, do not put pressure on those who may be hesitant to speak during the first few sessions. You may want to suggest the following guidelines to your group.

   • Stick to the topic being discussed.

   • Your responses should be based on the verses which are the focus of the discussion and not on outside authorities such as commentaries or speakers.

   • These studies focus on a particular passage of Scripture. Only rarely should you refer to other portions of the Bible. This allows for everyone to participate in in-depth study on equal ground.

   • Anything said in the group is considered confidential and will not be discussed outside the group unless specific permission is given to do so.

   • We will listen attentively to each other and provide time for each person present to talk.

   • We will pray for each other.

4. Have a group member read the introduction at the beginning of the discussion.

5. Every session begins with a group discussion question. The question or activity is meant to be used before the passage is read. The question introduces the theme of the study and encourages group members to begin to open up. Encourage as many members as possible to participate and be ready to get the discussion going with your own response.

   This section is designed to reveal where our thoughts or feelings need to be transformed by Scripture. That is why it is especially important not to read the passage before the discussion question is asked. The passage will tend to color the honest reactions people would otherwise give because they are, of course, supposed to think the way the Bible does.

   You may want to supplement the group discussion question with an icebreaker to help people to get comfortable. See the community section of the *Small Group Starter Kit* (IVP, 1995) for more ideas.

   You also might want to use the personal reflection question with your group. Either allow a time of silence for people to respond individually or discuss it together.

6. Have a group member (or members if the passage is long) read aloud the passage to be studied. Then give people several minutes to read the passage again silently so that they can take it all in.

7. Question 1 will generally be an overview question designed to briefly survey the passage. Encourage the group to look at the whole passage, but try to avoid getting sidetracked by questions or issues that will be addressed later in the study.

8. As you ask the questions, keep in mind that they are designed to be used just as they are written. You may simply read them aloud. Or you may prefer to express them in your own words.

   There may be times when it is appropriate to deviate from the study guide. For example, a question may have already been answered. If so, move on to the next question. Or someone may raise an important question not covered in the guide. Take time to discuss it, but try to keep the group from going off on tangents.

9. Avoid answering your own questions. If necessary, repeat or rephrase them until they are clearly understood. Or point out something you read in the leader's notes to clarify the context or meaning. An eager group quickly becomes passive and silent if they think the leader will do most of the talking.

10. Don't be afraid of silence. People may need time to think about the question before formulating their answers.

11. Don't be content with just one answer. Ask, "What do the rest of you think?" or "Anything else?" until several people have given answers to the question.

12. Acknowledge all contributions. Try to be affirming whenever possible. Never reject an answer. If it is clearly off-base, ask, "Which verse led you to that conclusion?" or again, "What do the rest of you think?"

13. Don't expect every answer to be addressed to you, even though this will probably happen at first. As group members become more at ease, they will begin to truly interact with each other. This is one sign of healthy discussion.

14. Don't be afraid of controversy. It can be very stimulating. If you don't resolve an issue completely, don't be frustrated. Move on and keep it in mind for later. A subsequent study may solve the problem.

15. Periodically summarize what the group has said about the passage. This helps to draw together the various ideas mentioned and gives continuity to the study. But don't preach.

16. At the end of the Bible discussion you may want to allow group members a time of quiet to work on an idea under "Now or Later." Then discuss what you experienced. Or you may want to encourage group members to work on these ideas between meetings. Give an opportunity during the session to allow people to talk about what they are learning.

17. Conclude your time together with conversational prayer, adapting the prayer suggestion at the end of the study to your group. Ask for God's help in following through on the commitments you've made.

18. End on time.

Many more suggestions and helps are found in *How to Lead a LifeBuilder Study*.

## Components of Small Groups

A healthy small group should do more than study the Bible. There are four components to consider as you structure your time together.

*Nurture.* Small groups help us to grow in our knowledge and love of God. Bible study is the key to making this happen and is the foundation of your small group.

*Community.* Small groups are a great place to develop deep friendships with other Christians. Allow time for informal interaction before and after each study. Plan activities and games that will help you to get to know each other. Spend time having fun together—going on a picnic or cooking dinner together.

*Worship and prayer.* Your study will be enhanced by spending time praising God together in prayer or song. Pray for each other's needs—and keep track of how God is answering prayer in your group. Ask God to help you to apply what you are learning in your study.

*Outreach.* Reaching out to others can be a practical way of applying what you are learning, and it will keep your group from becoming self-focused. Host a series of evangelistic discussions for your friends or neighbors. Clean up the yard of an elderly friend. Serve at a soup kitchen together, or spend a day working in the community.

Many more suggestions and helps in each of these areas are found in the *Small Group Starter Kit*. You will also find information on building a small group. Reading through the starter kit will be worth your time.

## Study 1. Learning to Obey. Luke 5:1–11.

*Purpose:* To see Simon Peter as a real human being who felt, thought and struggled with obedience just like us.

**Group discussion.** Be sure to have paper and pencils handy for this exercise. It may be necessary to encourage people to respect their "comfort zones" in terms of what they write, especially if this is a new group or a first study for some. Getting to know each other's spiritual histories and issues is important for a small group, but responses should be thoughtful, careful and not critical or mocking.

**Personal reflection.** This is designed to deepen and enhance one's memory of times when obedience to God has been particularly difficult or challenging. In a group, you may want to have a time of silent prayer to prepare for the Holy Spirit to be the teacher for the lesson that follows.

**Question 1.** A creative use of the imagination can help a study group look at a familiar passage of Scripture in a new way. Encourage the group to be "at the seaside." You may want to ask prompting questions, such as: What was the wind like? What sounds would be coming from the Lake of Gennesaret (also called the Sea of Galilee)? What were the people doing? The beach experiences of those in the group can help them feel the reality of this event.

Being in the boat would have amplified the sound. Being some distance from the crowd would have made Jesus more easily seen by all. If you want to bring this point out, you might ask, "Why do you think Jesus wanted to teach from Simon's boat (v. 3)?"

**Question 3.** The clear water of the lake made night fishing more profitable for netting fish. Note that it would naturally be hard for an expert fisherman like Peter to take advice about fishing from a traveling rabbi.

**Question 4.** Imagining ourselves in the scene is a helpful exercise in the study of Scripture. It reminds us how real these situations are and helps us better appreciate the actual responses of God and people's lives we study in the Word.

**Question 5.** The magnitude of this miracle in Simon Peter's area of expertise humbled him significantly.

**Question 6.** It is important to note that Jesus did not argue with Peter over the fact that he was a sinner. This was not news to Jesus! What is significant is that Jesus did not "depart" from this sinful man. God changes and works through sinful people—the only kind of people available.

**Question 8.** A good book to recommend to people intimidated by the idea of evangelism is *Speaking of Jesus* by J. Mack Stiles (InterVarsity Press).

**Question 10.** Don't overlook the financial impact of this catch. It could be difficult to leave such a windfall behind and not benefit directly from it. However, such a catch could also provide well for families left behind.

## Study 2. Learning to Pray. Mark 1:29–39; Luke 6:12–23.

*Purpose:* To see how prayer was the stabilizing force behind Jesus' ministry.

**Group discussion.** Extensive details are not important in this exercise. Just identify a major decision and how it was reached. Suggesting that the group consider how prayer, Scripture or the counsel of others was involved in the decision making-process may be helpful.

**Personal reflection.** This is designed to help in reflecting on decision-making patterns in one's life. Identifying the influences in decision-making can help one keep some and work to limit others.

**Question 2.** Encourage participants to reflect on the pressures they might feel to accommodate people or make sure things are done fairly. The group should reflect on how physically tiring and emotionally draining this might be.

**Question 5.** There may be several good suggestions concerning the burden of Jesus' prayer time on this day. Encourage the group to consider the situation in Simon's home when they arrived (1:29–31) and Jesus' intention to preach (1:38) after they departed.

**Question 6.** Encourage the group to focus on patterns or habits of prayer and not the "exceptional" prayer that brought forth a memorable answer. Habits of faithfulness are foundational in the Christian life as we learn to be like Jesus.

**Question 7.** *Apostle* means one *sent out* for a special purpose.

**Question 9.** Luke 6:17 describes the diverse group of people attracted to Jesus at this time. His fame was spreading. Note the contrast of this successful and powerful situation with the content of Jesus' sermon.

**Now or Later.** Keeping a prayer journal or creating a prayer log can help good prayer habits develop. *Daring to Draw Near* by John White (InterVarsity Press) is a good book to read because it looks at various prayers prayed by people in the Bible.

## Study 3. Learning to Trust. Matthew 14:22–34.

*Purpose:* To discover how to put our trust in God in the midst of circumstances that tempt us to rely on ourselves.

**Group discussion.** This can be an uncomfortable exercise for group participants who find it difficult to be honest about sin or failure. However, like Peter, learning to trust God with our recovery from failure is vital to spiritual maturity. It may help to remind the group of this before the discussion begins, in order to set an honest tone.

**Personal reflection.** Writing can often help our ability to think more slowly and therefore more deeply about things that affect our faith. Be as specific as possible in this exercise, noting how you felt as well as what you did. Writing a prayer to the Lord about these reflections can also be helpful.

**Question 1.** The feeding of the five thousand was a public miracle that stirred the crowds to adoration and manic expectations for Jesus as a rabbi and possible Messiah. You may want to read John 6:14–15, a parallel account of this miracle, to better understand the dynamics of the event. One possible reason Jesus may have had for sending the disciples away was to keep them from the temptations that come from power and prestige. Jesus also had to resist the temptation of a crowd-pleasing ministry with its seductive pull to worldly power. The event which is the focus of this study is actually a stark reminder of human frailty and a call to utterly trust God.

**Question 3.** The fourth watch of the night was between 3:00a.m. and 6:00a.m.

**Question 5.** There can be a variety of reasons suggested, from dealing with fear to trying to prove the reality of Jesus' presence. Help the group consider how these reasons are often the same ones we use in "testing" the Lord in trying circumstances.

**Question 10.** Worship is an exercise that helps "keep us in our place." We are needy, frail people and God is the only almighty One. Worship also draws us to the presence and steadfast love of the Lord, who forgives our failures and sin.

## Study 4. Learning to Believe. Matthew 16:13–25.

*Purpose:* To define who Jesus is in order to strengthen our belief and trust in him.

**Group discussion.** If your group has a number of seekers or new believers, you may want to do this in teams, pairing more mature believers with them. Let each person's summary stand without critique at this time.

**Question 1.** A Gentile woman called Jesus "Son of David" (Mt 15:21–28). Both the Sadducees and Pharisees, two very different Jewish political-religious parties, asked for a "sign from heaven" (Mt 16:1–4) to test Jesus. John, Elijah and Jeremiah were all teachers of the faithful who spoke out against those in political power.

**Question 3.** If there is a need to discuss the various historical understandings of Peter's declaration in Matthew 16:18, Ephesians 2:19–20 is a useful cross-reference to consider.

**Question 4.** It's important to help the group note all that Jesus includes in his comprehensive reply to Peter. Ask the group to note how Jesus moves from affirming *who* he (Jesus) is to defining *what* he will do. Then Jesus talks about who Peter is and what Peter will do.

**Question 5.** We do not know if Peter was biologically the son or descendant of someone named Jonah or if Jesus was referring to the prophet Jonah as Peter's spiritual father.

Acts 10 is the account of how the church was to be inclusive of believing Gentiles—a revelation given to Peter in the port city of Joppa. The Old Testament prophet Jonah escaped to Joppa by trying to avoid taking God's message to a Gentile city. The book which bears his name is the story of Jonah's resistance in sharing God's Word with non-Jews and the resulting consequences. It is interesting to consider the possibility that centuries later, in building the church, a descendant of Jonah will be obedient in welcoming all who believe to be the children of God in the kingdom of his Son.

The only other time Jesus includes Peter's lineage in addressing him is when he recommissions him after the resurrection as a disciple (Jn 21:15).

**Question 6.** Consider the turmoil surrounding the ministries of John, Elijah and Jeremiah. All were severely persecuted and denied public ministry for a time. Consider the part "timing" could have played in Jesus' admonition.

**Question 11.** Consider how you "set your mind" on various interests. How can this affect your insight into the things of God?

## Study 5. Learning to Follow. Matthew 17:1–8; 19:23–30.

*Purpose:* To discover that learning to follow Jesus means following him into suffering as well as to glory.

**Group discussion and personal reflection.** Some may recall Paul's declaration in Philippians that all things are to be counted loss for the sake of knowing Jesus. But noting the particulars of what is really costly, even though considered worth it, is valuable in our identity as disciples.

**Question 2.** The intensity of the experience would prove to be nearly too much for even Jesus' inner circle of disciples. The personal nature of Jesus' experience could only be shared with these few.

**Question 3.** The deaths of both Moses and Elijah are recorded in Scripture as unusual (Deut 34:1–8; 2 Kings 2:11–18). Both experienced their final moments in communication with the Lord, and both had disciples who searched in vain for their bodies. Could their unique experiences of death be comforting to Jesus at this time, as well as making their appearance possible in the physical realm?

**Question 4.** Try not to let the familiarity of this event keep the group from careful observation of this extraordinary passage. The overwhelming dynamics and reality of these things are reasons that Peter tried to gain some control by containing them in religious observance, ceremony and ritual.

**Question 5.** Consider in particular why God interrupts Peter at this point. Jesus is not to be confined or defined by religious ritual and commemoration.

**Question 7.** It can be helpful to discuss how you have seen situations, in your life or in the life of the church, in which the Lord is working powerfully and people attempt to control or contain what is happening. But don't allow this discussion to stray into a time of gossip, complaining or exercising a critical spirit.

**Question 9.** A variety of reactions are possible from regret to joy, skepticism to hope.

**Question 12.** It's one thing to say how we would have felt "in Jesus' day," but these words are just as true today and still make a claim on our lives in substantial ways. Make sure the group takes plenty of time to wrestle with what it costs and what is promised in learning to follow Jesus.

## Study 6. Learning to Serve. John 13:1–17.

*Purpose:* To discover that learning to serve is one thing that teaches us what it means to be like Jesus.

**Group discussion.** You may also want to use the personal reflection question if there is time.

**Personal reflection.** A willingness to be served is often a mark of security. Pride often makes us uncomfortable when others serve us.

**Question 1.** Make sure to note what Jesus knew at this time (vv. 1, 3). These are indications of what preoccupied his thinking on this night. To "love them to the end" was going to be painful and costly. The disciples were tired, tense and less than thoughtful in the threatening atmosphere of Jerusalem.

**Question 2.** In his humanity Jesus struggled in responding obediently to the work of the cross (Mk 14:36). It may have been difficult to look at these self–absorbed disciples and see them as the future self-sacrificing servants of the new kingdom. Jesus may have washed their dirty and dusty feet to remind himself of their simple humanity, and to practice his own patience with them until the Spirit came with transforming power. Jesus is showing his disciples what he has been trying to teach them.

**Question 4.** You may want to ask if this resistance is seen in our own lives.

**Question 5.** The "washing of entry" took place as guests entered a household and was usually done by the lowliest servant. It offered practical refreshment and an appropriately intimate welcome. Submission to this task was a symbol of accepting one's place in a household as an invited guest. Allowing one's feet to be washed was a privilege offered by grace, not a presumption of honor.

**Question 7.** See John 18:15–18, 25–27. Jesus also washed the feet of Judas knowing his betrayal was at hand.

**Question 9.** Jesus persisted in loving his disciples. This can show us a patience and perspective we need in learning to be like Jesus.

## Study 7. Learning to Love. John 13:31–14:4.

*Purpose:* To see love as the central character of Jesus and the central command of his ministry.

**Group discussion.** Be sure to have paper and pencils handy for this exercise. If there is time, after each person is identified, go around the room and ask the question suggested for personal reflection, but limit each person to the top two or three things.

**Question 2.** Jesus had only a few days left with his disciples prior to the resurrection, and his last week had been filled with loving works and words.

**Question 4.** It may be helpful to note what Peter did not question or comment on when Jesus spoke. The command of Jesus seems overshadowed by Peter's concern. What might this indicate about Peter's priorities?

**Question 5.** Discuss how the roots of confidence can be prideful and unrealistic. Counting the cost before investment was an important part of Jesus' teaching on discipleship.

**Question 6.** Include in your discussion Jesus' comments before and after the chapter breaks in the text.

**Question 8.** The chapter breaks in our Bibles have been artificially imposed and are not originally a part of the writing. Help the group see that Jesus' words in chapter 14 are a continuation of his words in chapter 13, so they will catch the fuller impact of what is taking place.

**Question 10.** Jesus told Peter the truth, but then followed it with words of grace. Speaking the truth in love is essential in learning to be like Jesus.

**Question 11.** It is good to bear in mind that although Peter would deny the Lord before sunrise, in the long run Peter would give his life for Jesus.

## Study 8. Learning to Persevere. Luke 22:54–62; 24:1–12.

*Purpose:* To emphasize the need for perseverance in the life of a Christian through the power of our resurrected Savior.

**Group discussion.** Encourage group members to be as specific as possible and help the group listen for common themes like "family," "those who are closest to us," "my boss at work." If there is time, you may want to ask, "Who are the easiest people to witness to and what are the most comfortable circumstances?"

**Question 1.** The Passover supper began near sundown with Jesus' time of prayer extending into the late evening. The trial of Jesus extended into the night; cocks begin to crow shortly before dawn (Lk 22:14, 39, 54–55, 61).

**Question 2.** Remind the group of Peter's promise at the end of John 13 from last week's study

**Question 5.** It may be helpful to ask the group to imagine, as if they were directing actors in a film, the expression on both Jesus' face and Peter's as the cock crowed. It is interesting that many churches in Europe have roosters on top of their steeples as a visual reminder to believers not to deny knowing Christ.

You may wonder how Jesus entered this scene (v. 61). According to the *NIV Study Bible*, "Peter was outside in the enclosed courtyard, and perhaps Jesus was being taken from the trial by Caiaphas to the Sanhedrin when Jesus caught Peter's eye" (Kenneth Barker, ed., Zondervan, 1995, p. 1582).

**Question 7.** If needed you can give this summary of the events surrounding the crucifixion:

After Jesus had appeared before the chief priests and elders, the guards mocked him and beat him. Then Jesus was handed over to Pilate in the early morning. As a political courtesy Pilate referred Jesus to Herod, the ruler of Galilee, who was in Jerusalem for the Passover. Herod sent Jesus back to Pilate, who had Jesus flogged even though no charges were proved against him. As a political favor for the religious leaders, Pilate gave Roman authority for the crucifixion of Jesus. Soldiers abused Jesus, mocked him and led him to Calvary, where he died.

It may be helpful to assign pairs (or individuals) one part of this list to act out or describe.

**Question 8.** The intensification of regrets and the profound longing to make things right can accelerate efforts to resolve the relationship or cause a person to give up and retreat from the relationship. It is interesting to note that after the resurrection Peter tended to do both in attempting to deal with his guilt. The next study will reflect on the latter.

## Study 9. Learning to Start Again. John 21:1–19.

*Purpose:* To recognize the grace offered through Jesus' love that allows us to start over after failure and to see through Peter's life how God's mercy is "new every morning" (Lam 3:22–23).

**Group discussion.** Identifying how people usually deal with insecurity or the aftermath of failure can help the group realize how very human Peter was in his efforts to stay busy doing what was familiar.

**Question 1.** Consider that Jesus chose a comfortable and familiar place to recommission Peter for ministry. Jesus did not revisit the courtyard to help Peter deal with his failure; Jesus met Peter at the seashore.

**Question 2.** References to Peter's initial call to follow Jesus may be helpful. Study one in this guide used Luke 5:1–11, but the story is also found in Matthew 4:18–22 and Mark 1:16–20.

**Question 4.** Recall the threefold denial and consider Jesus' insight into Peter's need to declare his fidelity. Notice also that they seem to be alone—perhaps walking on the beach. (Verse 20 says another disciple followed him.) Notice how Jesus initiated this walk. Jesus did not have this conversation with Peter in front of the other disciples.

**Question 6.** Peter was learning that faithfulness is a lot harder than fishing. To follow Jesus is a costly decision. It was tempting for Peter to settle for success as a fisherman rather than risk failure again as a disciple.

**Question 7.** It may be helpful to ask the group what word, *agape* or *phileo*, Peter might have used in expressing his love to Jesus at the end of John 13 when he declared, "I will lay down my life for you!" How much is Peter willing to promise Jesus now?

Discuss why Jesus changed his word for "love" in his third question to match Peter's. How would this contribute to the reconciliation between Jesus and Peter?

**Question 8.** Jesus knew the frailty of Peter's love. It was Peter who needed to recognize his limits and begin to follow Jesus more honestly and humbly.

**Question 10.** It is interesting to note that Peter's brash declaration in John 13 is Jesus' prophecy for him in John 21:19. The heroic offer of the young disciple became an act of obedient faith on the part of the older apostle.

## Study 10. Learning to Witness. Acts 3:1–20.

*Purpose:* To understand that the Christian witness is essentially an eye-witness account of how the work of Jesus on the cross and in the resurrection changes lives.

**Group discussion.** Encourage the group members to summarize the events they share. This can be a wonderful celebration of God's faithfulness. Those still seeking a relationship with Jesus often have something to share too.

**Personal reflection.** Giving thanks to the Lord for how your life has changed by knowing Jesus can be a joyous exercise.

**Question 1.** The three stated times of prayer for Jews were 9:00a.m., 3:00p.m. and sunset. The "gate called Beautiful" was a major entrance to the temple court. The initial ministry of the disciples was to practicing Jews—people much like themselves.

**Question 2.** Acts 4:22 reveals that this beggar was over forty years old when he was healed. This man at the gate called Beautiful was a familiar sight. Everybody knew this man and his plight. They had passed him countless times.

**Question 3.** Have group members identify similar people in their own communities—the disabled man in front of a popular grocery store, the blind lady at the post office. This discussion can help the group grasp the impact of this familiar story in a new way. If a disabled person your community was suddenly and publicly healed, what would happen?

**Question 4.** Part of Peter's audience didn't like what he preached. The Sadducees were a Jewish religious-political party fairly tolerant of Roman occupation. In contrast to the Pharisees, they denied the possibility of the resurrection of the dead. It was the Sadducees who had Peter arrested after the man was healed and the sermon delivered.

**Question 5.** Focus on Peter's comment in verse 15—the resurrection of Jesus was the issue being disputed. The Greek word translated *witnesses* in Acts 1:8 and 3:15 includes the specific idea of an eyewitness—one who relates a firsthand account, not someone else's vicarious experience. It is interesting to note that the English word *martyr* is a derivation of the Greek word for witness.

**Question 6.** *Handbook of Christian Apologetics* by Peter Kreeft and Ron Tacelli (InterVarsity Press) is an excellent resource for such questions.

**Question 10.** Have group members share their testimonies with one another in pairs.

**Question 11.** Peter was in a hostile place to talk about resurrection. The Sadducees (vv. 1–2) were a powerful presence in Jerusalem and the temple in particular.

**Question 14.** It is notable that the disciples did not pray against those who were persecuting them, but only for their own faithfulness and God's continuing work among them.

## Study 11. Learning to Change. Acts 9:36–10:48.

*Purpose:* To show the difficulties that even the most faithful followers of Jesus face in overcoming prejudice and in crossing cultural boundaries, and to show the faithfulness of God's work in his servants to overcome all "walls" between the people he loves.

**General note.** Ephesians 2:11–16 discloses God's purposes for the gospel and his heart for the reconciliation of all people to each other as well as to himself.

The lesson of Acts 10 is pivotal for understanding salvation and the gospel message. Be especially prayerful in leading the group through this study.

**Group discussion.** Encourage the group to be honest and specific about barriers of prejudice that hinder our relationship with other people and our lives as ambassadors of Christ.

**Personal reflection.** Be as specific as you can in identifying an area of prejudice or racism in your life. People keep other people at arm's length for reasons ranging from obesity to political affiliation, from immoral practices to petty differences.

**Question 2.** In the few instances in Scripture where Jesus brought the dead back to life (for instance Lk 7:14–15; 8:54–55), Jesus *touched* the dead person in raising them up. However, Peter's behavior could be indicative of his lifelong care in keeping the Jewish law. This will be seen even more clearly in Acts 10.

**Questions 3–4.** Contact with a tanner without elaborate cleansing rituals would have been prohibited. The fact that Scripture records where Peter stayed in a city is rare, and its significance should be considered. (Usually just the name of the city is mentioned.) From the raising of Tabitha to staying in the home of this tanner to the events which lead to the Gentiles, God is preparing Peter to cross boundaries and forsake long-held prejudice he never imagined.

Consider how difficult it is for a long-held taboo or custom to be changed in your life. It may help if the group reflects on examples in their own experiences. These can range from embedded ethnic prejudices to cooking customs to the "right way" to fold laundry or wash a car.

**Question 7.** Joppa was considered a "free city" in Roman-occupied Palestine. No Roman garrison was stationed there, so prejudice against Romans and Gentiles in this proud Jewish city would have been high. Note that the messengers inquired about Peter at the outer gate, not venturing beyond that point. Take careful note of verse 22 and the words used to deliver the message. Ethnically, culturally and socially this encounter was unique!

**Question 8.** In the original text the person extending the invitation for these visitors to enter is ambiguous. It would be most likely that the homeowner, Simon the tanner, would be the one to extend this invitation—especially in this situation where cultural and religious traditions were being violated. "Pharisaic opinions avoided tanners whenever possible, because their stripping of animal hides continually involved them with unclean carcasses. Second-century teachers reported (not necessarily accurately) that tanners had been forbidden in Jerusalem (many rabbis were more lenient if the tannery were near water, as Simon's house is–10:6)" (Craig Keener, *The IVP Bible Background Commentary: New Testament*, InterVarsity Press, 19, p. 349).

**Question 11.** In Acts 11:12 we are told that six Jewish brothers accompanied Peter to Cornelius's home. Roman law required seven witnesses to establish a fact. This story is told completely three times in the book of Acts. It was so unexpected and so unbelievable that the church had to hear this story over and over to "get it."

## Study 12. Learning to Learn. Acts 15:1–12; Galatians 2:11–16.

*Purpose:* To see how much we need the accountability of a community of God's people to help us learn to be like Jesus and to see that discipleship is not instant.

**General note.** Holding each other accountable in grace as well as in truth is a real gift of Christian community. A good book to read for more information on this topic is Eugene Peterson's *Perseverance: A Long Obedience in the Same Direction* (Leicester: IVP, 1996).

**Group discussion.** This can be a good "closing" exercise for this study of Simon Peter as the group looks ahead to what to study next.

**Personal reflection.** Sometimes it is more difficult or challenging to be the one who holds another person accountable. Keeping both grace and truth active in the process is essential.

**Question 2.** Peter listened carefully to the debate in the context of his own experience with the Gentiles and his ethnic heritage and upbringing. Peter thought it through before he spoke.

**Question 5.** Take care that the discussion stays within appropriate bounds and that there is no breach of confidentiality or gossip. As a leader, you may have to hold someone accountable.

**Question 6.** Peter's beliefs were correct (Acts 15), but his behavior was hypocritical. The book of Galatians was written to expose people in the early church who felt Gentiles must become Jews before they became Christians. It was hard for many Jews to turn their backs on the rituals and traditions that they had been taught all their lives. It would be like discovering something you always thought was "bad" for you (sugar, caffeine or not washing your hands before dinner) was really quite all right, even "good" for you. On a much more significant scale, Gentiles were suddenly okay—and lifelong practices and prejudices didn't change easily for many.

**Question 9.** Help the group be practical and concrete in discussing this question.

**Now or Later.** Keep this enjoyable—a celebration of the study's conclusion.

*Robbie Castleman is Professor Emerita Theology and New Testament, John Brown University, Siloam Springs, Arkansas. She is the author of* Parenting in the Pew *and* True Love in a World of False Hope *(InterVarsity Press).*